Sarah Liebstein

A LITTLE

DATING GUIDE

Bibliographic information published by the Deutsche Nationalbibliothek
The Deutsche Nationalbibliothek lists this publication in the Deutsche Nationalbibliografie; detailed bibliographic data are available on the internet: http://dnb.dnb.de

Printed and published by: BoD - Books on Demand, Norderstedt/ Germany
ISBN Nr. 978-3-7543-00701

Dear Michaela, I would like to say thank you.
Thank you for your inspiration, help and support.
And also for your uncountable lovely and uplifting
words.

Contents

Contents I

Introduction 11

Chapter One 16

Since When Has Dating Become So Difficult? 16

    Dating nowadays 19

    The fear of commitment.....................................22

Chapter Two.. 28

Being Happily Single Before Starting a Relationship 28

    Why do we lack self-love? 31

    Building self-love and confidence....................35

Chapter Three 42

Your Vibe Attracts Your Tribe 42

    Introducing the law of attraction 44

    Attracting the things you want........................48

Chapter Four 53

Where Do I Find Love?.. 53

    Your community 56

    The complex debate of dating at the workplace.............59

    Approaching women in public..........................64

    What about online dating?...............................67

Chapter Five 71

Approaching Others... 71

   Is your shyness hindering you from potential dates? 73

   How *not* to approach a woman 76

   When should I message her? How often?.......................82

Chapter Six 88

The First Date.. 88

   Picking the location 90

   Dating 101...94

   Dealing with rejection..100

   Rejecting others respectfully 103

Chapter Seven 107

What If It's Over?... 107

   Is it time to call it off?..109

   Breaking it off nicely 113

   I was dumped, how do I gain my confidence back?......115

Conclusion 119

Introduction

Imagine this: you're sitting down at a café, waiting for Emilie, or Émile, or Jack, or whoever it is... The clock is ticking, your coffee is getting cold, and you keep refreshing your tinder messages every thirty seconds, hoping to see "I'm just running a couple of minutes late", but it doesn't seem to appear at the top of the screen. You wonder to yourself, what have you done that would make your date just not want to show up? Was it something you said? Or did they see you in the window and bolt? Whatever is the reason, it's enough to make one wonder if they'll ever be able to find someone. There's something really painful in rejection, but it's even worse when you don't know what the reason is. However, in this day and age, it's something we have become accustomed to.

Relationships, partnerships, dating... Whatever you may want to call it, nowadays, it has drastically changed. What used to be all about being romantic, has become a game of matches, speed dating and going through dozens of dates every year in the hopes of finding *the one*. But the question remains: how has dating changed? What is so drastically different, and why has this become the case? And, most importantly, how do we successfully find a partner in this new dating society?

Over the course of our time together, I will guide you through the art of dating nowadays. Throughout a series of anecdotes, personal stories (yes, bad dating experiences occur to *everybody)*, as well as straightforward facts and tips, you will hopeful finish this book with increased knowledge and a new confidence regarding dating. After all, finding love shouldn't be so hard! So we will look at this. Building confidence for a successful dating experience. How do you build your confidence? How do you learn to love yourself, and do you *actually* need to love yourself before being able to love anybody else?

Not only will I guide you through this, but I will additionally discuss the law of attraction, as it's true that your vibe attracts your tribe. Do you know about this law? It has been used by countless people to find what they want most; whether this is money or love. It is one that is easy to follow, but you must develop the right mindset for it. I have used it a few times in my life and have found it is a great tool.

In fact, this book will go in depth on a number of things. For example, can you find love anywhere? And, an important question: should you go into a relationship that is built at work? It can be seriously confusing to start having feelings for a coworker, and how do you decide whether or not to keep going? I know I've been in this situation before, and it's a tough one to navigate. Additionally, I will also give you tips on where to find love, including apps, but mostly how to find it outside, in real life! It *is* possible. Later on, you will also find out more about how to approach women and/or men, and I will address the very real problems that we face as a society with regard to dating. If your love life has been somewhat unsuccessful, this might be because of the place and ways you approach women, namely these may not be the greatest. For example, although you may be a great guy, any man that approaches a woman at one in the morning in a dark street is bound to be rejected– it's a normal reaction!

Of course, a book discussing relationships would not be complete if we didn't mention how to live in a successful relationship, and in the unfortunate case that it wouldn't last, how to become happily single once we break up with someone, or are broken up with. We will talk about commitment and responsibilities; what happens when the relationship lasts quite long? What about kids? Marriage? How do you deal with all of this? My hope with this book is that you are able to feel like you have gained a lot of knowledge, meanwhile, without feeling like you are reading a robot! Dating is a personal thing, and I feel that we often forget that, after all, we are all just human beings trying to find love. We all make mistakes, we are all different and have varying cultures that make us act in a certain way or another.

So, this is what I will share with you, and this is all based on my experience as a woman who has dated quite a bit!

Now, without further ado, let me tell you about my very first experience dating.

Chapter One

Since When Has Dating Become So Difficult?

When I first started dating, around the age of nineteen or twenty(of course, I did have a few girlfriends in the past, but I was not one of the lucky ones that had a long-lasting high school relationships...), I plunged into the dating pool head first and started looking around for whatever I could find. I was struck by this need for love, for attention, for caring from someone, and that meant I was ready to look pretty much everywhere to find it. I know it may sound desperate, but what can I say. It happened! First going to bars, to clubs, and I know what you're thinking– who goes to a club to find love? Well, I felt as if the world had somehow changed. What had happened to the dating we see in old vintage movies? What happened to writing letters, to courting someone, to bring them out to dinner first? I was shocked to see first-hand that the game had turned around– now, dating to find a relationship is rare, and commitment is a word many are afraid of.

So, being nineteen or twenty and looking for something serious, you can imagine the stories I have. From meeting guys that were absolutely appalled to hear that I was looking for something serious, to being stood up on dates, or, what they nowadays call "*ghosted*", I had my fair share of downsides. I recall the exact time I stood in a restaurant, looking forward to meeting my date, and him calling me to say he "just didn't feel like it tonight"– don't get me wrong, it's absolutely alright to not feel like going out, but could you not have at least told me before I was sitting down at the restaurant? And, before you ask, no I wasn't there hours early!

So *why* has dating become this difficult? What has changed over the past decades? Well, many things have changed– from family forms, to the value of marriage, to the general expectation regarding relationships, and to the new opportunities online dating has brought to us, we date significantly differently than the previous generations did. Let's have an in-depth look at how each of the latters have changed.

Dating nowadays

First, family forms have radically changed. What used to be the norm, or nuclear families consisting of a father, a mother, and a few children, has now become somewhat of a rarity depending on where you live. In the United States and Canada, single, adoptive, and same-sex parents and couples have become a new norm; something that would have been an absolute scandal just a century ago. Now, as mentioned, this differs depending on where you live. If you reside in the United States, Canada or Great Britain, or any similar country you may relate to this fully, however if we compare this new family form to the family form in, let's say, rural Kenya, the residents there may have quite a hard time trying to understand just what we mean by a single-parent family, or gay parents. Just think about you and your friends; how many of them are married? Compare this to the past, how drastically different is it?

And just why has this changed? One could indeed blame it on the lower importance given to religion, which is making people less likely to get married. Or perhaps this is because we are now growing increasingly used to being alone. In a day and age with more access than ever to different platforms and apps, and with more people to choose from with a growing population, it is quite special to see that family forms are changing. One could also blame the cost of raising a family– raising children is expensive! With school and university fees, the cost of houses, food, of all the sports clubs and dancing classes, and *so many clothes to buy* as the children grow up, and this is excluding all of the supplies one needs for children, many have started questioning whether or not it's really worth it to have children. If I listen to the youth explain this to me, their reasoning is simple: why should they use their hard-earned money for a child if they barely make enough to cover their own needs? And why give up their freedom and freetime to take care of a child? Naturally this sounds like quite a shallow or selfish, but one must consider the changes in the labour market, wages, and the general living costs before making a judgement. It's becoming harder to find a good job, and meanwhile, living is getting more expensive, so it's normal that people are growing more individualistic, less caring of others.

Alongside this new family form, marriage and all it entails have also drastically changed. Looking back to approximately a century ago, in the United States, more than two-thirds of persons aged fourteen and up were married! This would be absolutely shocking nowadays, namely due to the fact that it is illegal in many countries. This being said, why have we stopped getting married? As this trend– lowering averages of married couples– is a common trend in various countries, there must be a common factor. One could argue that this is due to the general decrease in the importance given to religion which is making people believe less in marriage. Another reason for this is the economic aspect of marriage– nowadays with women working much more than they used to, many couples have decided to avoid getting married to feel economically stuck. However, in certain countries, such as Germany, married couples are at an advantage as they pay less taxes than their non-married counterparts. Thus, this leaves room for debate. Another common reason stated for this drop in the marriage rate is the fact that women are becoming more educated and are working more, thus are becoming more specific about whom they decide to marry. Finally, another reason often given is the simple fact that many find marriage to be outdated and unnecessary. With rising mortgage prices, student loans and the incessant needs for credit cards in certain countries, some believe that marriage, including a wedding and all it requires, is a serious waste of money.

The fear of commitment

Talking about marriage; it's a serious commitment, which is another difference found between today's dating scene and that found decades ago. It's no secret: we have become scared of commitment. Whether it is because we are generally growing further apart from one another (did you know that the current generation of twenty-year olds is one of the loneliest ever documented?) or because we have too many other commitments that we do not want to add another to the list, our views regarding relationships, more specifically long-term, committed relationships, have significantly changed. We are afraid of commitment because of varying reasons; one of them being the fear of finding something better– a real problem in our society. For example, if you are swiping back and forth, left and right on Tinder, the likelihood is that you don't feel like you have to give it your all for one specific person, simply because there are many other options available. Similarly, nowadays many are worried that while they are on one date, they could be missing out on another, or a better one. How do you know if you aren't missing *the one* for a bad date? Do you want to take that chance? What if this other person is gone, or what if you do go to this other person, just to find out that you chose the wrong one? So many decisions!

I remember when I first used Tinder; it was so exciting! For the first time, it was easier than going up to guys in bars or trying to approach them in the streets without worrying about rejection. It's simple, if he likes me too, he'll swipe right and we will match. Then, I just need to send a witty message and hope for the best. However, I also realised that this was almost getting addictive. I would have phases every week or so where I would be refreshing my Tinder account, hopeing for new matches, and started becoming *very* picky. If Martin said something that I thought sounded weird, I would unmatch him, completely forgetting that this is a *person* I'm talking to, and not just a bot. That's one of the problems I see with such apps– the human connection is lost in some cases, and we become too rational, almost forgetting that the goal of such apps is to create connections... quite paradoxical, if you ask me. Sometimes I really regret the way I used these apps as I started seeing it as a game, and less as actually trying to find someone to date... But I will tell you more about this in the fourth chapter, when we talk about dating apps.

So you might wonder what I did to change this way of treating others? Simply said, I created a rule for myself: explain to my matches why I thought it would not work between us instead of just unmatching them away. This, in my eyes, was the minimum respect I owed them. After all, these guys are people with real feelings, and they at least deserve that. In any case, I realised that I was not ready to use such an app, or maybe it just was not my thing. I was ready to commit but was not ready to put in the work for it, or to even try things out, as the second a problem popped up I would just "unmatch the problem". You can't simply do that in life, just erase the problem if it pops up, so why do we allow ourselves to do this online?

A similar issue to commitment is that we are now less able to deal with vulnerability. We are generally more afraid of failure, of rejection, than ever before. This may be due to a variety of factors, namely, for example, social media which may be at fault for making us feel like there is always someone better looking, more intelligent, or richer than us out there. Thus, human beings being proud and fueling on pride, we may avoid commitment altogether just to avoid having our egos hit badly. Commitment is something we fear due to other factors alongside constantly looking for something better and avoiding vulnerability– for example, we have unrealistic expectations. As mentioned above, we live in a world with a lot of choice. We can swipe away someone we find unattractive, unmatch someone that isn't living up to what their profile promises, and have multiple dating apps to opt for in case one does not work out. This, therefore, also means that we have expectations that exceed what past generations had; finding the big love is the goal, but this comes with finding someone educated, with similar goals, who is attractive, who has the same values and beliefs as you do, and so on. For example, I might expect a potential date to offer all of the aforementioned aspects, but how does this work in real life? This is difficult to do! However, as we have endless choices and aren't bound to a specific location anymore, not only do we have constant new choices and people available, but we can look around the world, thereby allowing us to have high expectations. And, it makes sense: why would you commit and settle for someone that only ticks half of your boxes, while you *think* you may be able to find something better somewhere else? What has happened to loving other people's defects and imperfections? Food for thought...

Alongside all of these, time and space have changed the way our societies work with dating. We work more (have you heard of burnout?), have less free time, and meanwhile try to keep it together while taking care of the basics; paying rent, groceries, and so on. So, why would one want to add a person in this mix? As we work an increasing number of hours, the person you decide to dedicate a good part of your time to should at least be worth it– bringing us back to the past two points. Additionally, not only do we have less time, but we move around a lot. We travel or completely move to different countries every couple of months. Look at digital nomads or permanent travelers, how does one explain to someone that they aren't ready to settle down in a country but are looking for a real, committed relationship? If someone moves across the world every year or so, it can be very difficult to finding someone that is willing to live with that. I just need to think about the past few months of my life: I've travelled to Greece for two months, then Morocco for work, and then came to Germany for the summer. How should I explain this to a potential partner, and can I expect that they will want to be a part of this? If they want children or a stay-at-home wife, I am probably not the best bachelorette.

This being said, there is still hope. Indeed, the dating scene has significantly changed in the past few years, but on the positive side, it allows us to have a much vaster choice of people to choose from. We are no longer forced to stay within our circle of friends, or friends or relatives. It is now acceptable to marry or date someone from a different social class, something that would have also been scandalous a century ago. We can look in different countries, find love across the world, or stay in touch with someone we fell in love with while across the world. These new dating standards are different, yes, but they aren't *necessarily* bad. So what now? What's the next step in developing a healthy relationship? We've talked about the problems, so let's discuss solutions! But before anything else, the most important: what you need for a happy relationship, is to be happy with yourself first.

Chapter Two

Being Happily Single Before Starting a Relationship

Now that we have looked into how dating, relationships and families differ, let's talk about another very important part of dating: being happily single before going in for a relationship. Your friends that find themselves in relationships may have told you *"just wait, you see, I found someone when I stopped looking"*, and you may be very frustrated by this, but it's unfortunately true very often. Thus, it's vital that you learn how to be happily single before you are actually ready for a relationship.

Now you may ask yourself why this is important; and that's what I'm here to tell you. Have you ever been on a date with someone (or dated someone) that is negative, or that exudes a lack of confidence? Or, have you ever been on a date with someone that just seemed to want to go too fast (*"this date was great! What are you doing tomorrow? And the day after that? And the day after that?"*)? This is usually something that takes you aback, or something that actually makes you want to take a step back, as too much of anything is a bit worrying at first. This person is most likely so tired of being single that they're ready to find anybody, just to get that feeling of care and love. If that's your case, it's not necessarily a problem, but it's a sign that you have some work to do on yourself before getting together with someone else.

It's simple: you should not feel the need to have someone in your life to feel like you are successful, or to feel fulfilled with your life. Before you are able to settle down, your life and your own person must feel fulfilled and must feel like it's enough. No amount of caring or love coming from another person can make up for a lack of self-love and confidence. And don't worry, this is something we all go through!

Why do we lack self-love?

When I was nineteen years old, I had an epiphany when I realized that I really did not like who I was; I was unhappy with the way I looked, with what I was doing with my life, and with where it was going. I was dating the wrong people for what I was looking for; people that only wanted the fun part of dating, meanwhile I was looking for caring and love. I woke up one morning, having come back from a date that had ended up in a club that ended not-so-well, and realized that it was time I worked on myself. I deleted all my dating apps and started hitting the gym daily, reading more, learning a new language, and I ultimately became proud of myself for the way I had picked myself up. I became the happiest single out there; and why? Because I had finally realized that no one could fill the void that I felt when I woke up; a void that was due to a general unhappiness with my life and where it was going.

So how do you love yourself? What a loaded question. Loving yourself, being more confident and having a higher self esteem are all interconnected. Thus, I have prepared a few tips that can guide you through the art of developing self love. However, let's start by looking at the main reasons as to *why* we do not like who we are, as a first step to any solution is to point out the problem.

First, we compare ourselves too much to others, and this on a daily basis. While we scroll down Instagram, watch YouTube videos or use Facebook, or when we speak to family members and friends about what they have accomplished (or not) so far, we evaluate ourselves and our actions in regards to what others are or do numerous times. An example? Simply think of how many times you used your phone or any other mobile device to look up videos such as vlogs or travel diaries, or the last time you saw a "transformation video" showcasing a woman having lost a ton of weight. What was the outcome of doing this? Did it leave you feeling better about yourself, or did you question whether this was *better* than your transformation, or the travels you did. Comparing yourself to others often brings nothing but unhappiness as most of the time, these comparisons are negative; I wish I was more this, I wish I could do this better, and so on. Whether you compare your body to another person's, or how successful you would say you are, these comparisons are most often pessimistic and influence your self-esteem in a negative way.

A second reason why we have a hard time loving ourselves is the belief that we are not reaching our full potential. For example, if you constantly feel like you are not doing enough, or like you do not even know where to start to achieve your goals, you may feel like you are not reaching your full potential. Similarly, if you believe that you cannot reach this potential, maybe because you have a hard time believing in yourself overall, or because you receive too much negative feedback whenever you attempt to do something, this can seriously impact your self esteem. The opposite is also true; your self esteem is impacting how much you believe you *can* do.

The third reason, and this ties in well with the previous two, is that you may feel like you have no real goals to strive for. We humans are a simple species, we require a certain goal to move forward. If we are unable to see any end in sight, or if we are stuck in the same, repetitive routine, it can be seriously discouraging.

Now, these three reasons are often at the center of the reason why we do not love ourselves. This being said, how do we change this? How do you go from being unhappy and not loving yourself enough to being content and proud? There are a few steps, so let's start with the basics.

Building self-love and confidence

At the root of happiness are your basic needs, also known as the "Hierarchy of Needs" introduced by psychologist Abraham Maslow. This pyramid looks somewhat like this:

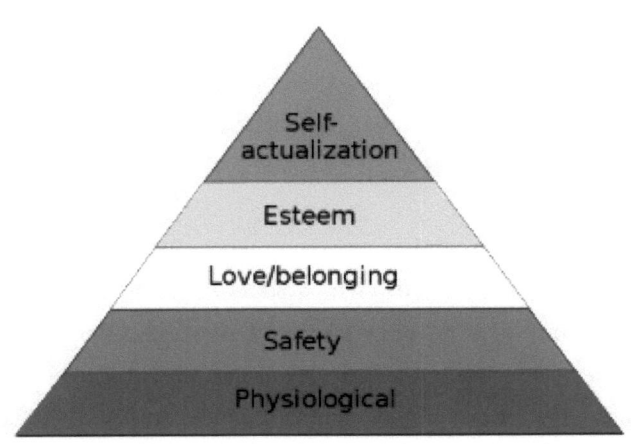

Source: https://en.wikipedia.org/wiki/Maslow%27s_hierarchy_of_needs

At the very bottom, you have your physiological needs, followed by safety, then feeling loved and like you belong to a community, then esteem, and once these are all fulfilled you reach self-actualization. For the physiological need fulfillment, you need the very basics; clean food, clean water and clean air. Being safe refers to being healthy and feeling safe where you are, for example, not feeling like you could potentially be killed at the step of your door. Love and belonging to a community means just this; feeling like you are a part of a certain community. The latter three allow you to have a certain amount of self esteem, and brought all together, these four make you a self-actualized person. Therefore, before you start working on loving yourself more on a deeper level, you must make sure to have the basics. Once this is done, you can move onto the next step. Here is a step-by-step online to help you develop your confidence, and to love yourself more.

First, you must start exercising more. Indeed, when you move your body more often, it starts releasing endorphins, also known as the "happy hormone". Nowadays, most office jobs are very sedentary– we walk around very little. Thus, it's important that you take some time every day to move around. For example, when I am having a horrible day, I know that it's the perfect time to go to the gym. Going home and being lazy on the couch will simply make me feel worse because I will feel like I have done absolutely nothing all day. However, if I go to the gym, even if everything else went wrong during that day, at least I know that I have achieved *this*. If you have never done sports before and don't know how to start, sign up at a gym that offers trials and potential trainers. Or, you could also sign up for a gym that offers classes. If you prefer training in groups, join a sports team; not only does this give you some social time outside of your office team, but it also keeps you accountable for showing up.

Your body needs two things to feel good: to move enough and to be fed real, nutritious food. You only have one body, so take good care of it. Stay away from foods that are heavily processed, or which contain high amounts of sugars and fats. On the same line of ideas, make sure to reach your daily recommendations regarding vitamins and minerals, these are extremely important to feel energized! I suggest that you start incorporating more fresh foods into your diet. For example, instead of having an energy drink, why not make a green smoothie instead? Or, instead of going out for lunch and having some fried noodles, opt for the salad, or better yet, make your own. Not only will this help you financially but I can guarantee you will have much more energy throughout the day.

You can also learn to love yourself more by being more selective about what you allow in your mind. For example, try to limit the number of hours that you spend in front of the TV watching reality TV or other similar shows. Of course, it's normal to spend some time relaxing by watching some TV shows, but cut out anything that leaves you feeling worse about yourself. This, therefore, also includes cutting out the negativity that social media brings. For example, if you find yourself feeling worse every time you open up a social media app and look at a certain influencer's page, unfollow them, it's that simple! Or, if your old high school classmate keeps posting self-involved posts about how perfect their life is, and if these make you question yourself (think back of the "comparing ourselves to others too often" part at the beginning of this chapter), cut it out of your life by blocking such posts from appearing on your feed. At the end of the day, it's okay to be a bit selfish when it comes to developing self-love, as no one can do it for you!

When you spend less time on these apps and watching pointless TV shows, you are able to get more rest and therefore more energy to do the things that you are passionate about, or, the things you have always wanted to try but were never able to find the time for. Therefore, if you have always wanted to start playing basketball weekly, or if you've been wanting to practice a language you studied in college, this is the time to do it. Concentrate on activities and creating goals that make you feel fulfilled and give you a sense of accomplishment. This is a form of self-care, which is another important aspect of life we often forget to do. Self-care differs from one person to the next; maybe your favourite self-care method is meditation, and for others it is to take time daily to go on a walk. Another form of self-care is noting down your accomplishments to look back at them in the future, or on bad days. For example, if going to the gym every second day is a great accomplishment for you, make sure to write it down, as it's great to look back on it on a day where you feel somewhat badly about yourself. It could also be a way to motivate yourself to go to the gym!

My final tip is to concentrate your time and energy on meaningful relationships with others. If you waste your time on relationships that are draining and holding you back from improving as a person, this is time and energy you are wasting that could go into another better, more fulfilling relationship.

Thus, here are a few things you should take from this;

1. Take care of your body, you only have one. Nourish and cherish it.
2. Be careful about what you allow in your mind; cut out all negativity and concentrate on only allowing in positivity.

3.   Use your time wisely on people and activities that fulfill you and make you feel accomplished. Cut out negativity, even if this means that you may have to leave an old friend behind. Not all friendships are meant to last.

By following the tips I have shared with you, you should be able to develop self-love to an extent where you are starting to feel much more confident in your own skin. Indeed, feeling confident usually follows self-love simply because one is almost impossible without the other. Confidence refers to the way you portray yourself to others, and how certain you are of yourself as a person, and this is directly influenced by how you really see and *appreciate* yourself. By loving yourself and working on your confidence as a whole, you should be getting better at being happily single.

Being happily single, however, is not all about being confident. It's also about knowing that your past experiences will not determine your future dating stories. You may have had a horrible experience with an ex and may be absolutely unable to imagine yourself in a relationship again. The only thing to keep in mind when this happens is that time heals. Most of us have had bad experiences with dating; some that have left us heartbroken and feeling empty, but this is not a reason to give up on love altogether. Work on bettering yourself and building up your confidence and give it time. Additionally, being single isn't synonymous with being miserable. Think about it– it's often better for your wallet (no need to pay for dates, transportation to your lover's house...), you get better sleep, more freedom with your sex partners and more freedom in general as you don't have someone waiting for you at home. As with anything in life, your perspective on the matter and how optimistic you are about it plays a major role in the events and people you attract– that's the law of attraction, and it will be discussed in the next chapter.

Chapter Three

Your Vibe Attracts Your Tribe

The Law of Attraction: a concept that has been gaining in popularity over the past few years. But, what it is, and what does it have to do with relationships and dating? In the simplest of terms, the Law of Attraction refers to a concept or belief that we can manifest (or attract) good things; whether that is money, love, fame, and so on, using positive affirmations. This law works for a number of life's spheres; it can help you generate more income, can bring you great friends, and can also bring you love. Recently, this law has been used widely by many young people and older generations alike in order to attract what they wish most; mostly money and love. This is actually more of a mindset, one in which you strongly believe that you deserve these things, and therefore you attract them. It's quite simple: if you are positive, and work hard, you will get what you deserve. Thus, in this chapter, we will look into this law; how it works and how you can use it to find love, as it's a really great tool!

Introducing the law of attraction

So you may be wondering, in what ways is this law related to dating? Well, simply explained, you can attract love using this law. However, the goal of this book is not to teach you how to use the law, but to make a point regarding attracting people that are similar to you– if you are very negative, you will most likely attract people with a similar mindset. If you are a very bubbly, positive and open-minded person, your vibe will attract your tribe. This works for love as well as for friendships.

Think about the kind of person you enjoy spending time with; are they very humorous? Are they open-minded? Are they extroverted, or introverts? What do they like to do; maybe they enjoy doing sports, or maybe they prefer sitting and chatting over coffee. Think about these people and their personal traits. Are these similar to your traits, and to the things you like to do? Probably, otherwise you most likely wouldn't enjoy spending time with them. The law works in a similar fashion; you will attract things you want by manifesting them, or by thinking consciously about what you are seeking.

Now, in concrete terms, how does one use the law of attraction to find love? Before looking at how to find love, let's take a look at what you have to be conscious of beforehand. There are a few things that could hinder from finding it, such as the following:

> **You have unconsciously shut yourself down after being disappointed and hurt from a past relationship.** It is normal behavior to protect one's self from further negative feelings that can come back. However, that also makes you unable to find potential further love. For example, if you were previously in a very difficult relationship that was either toxic or that left you feeling completely heartbroken, it is completely human to close yourself off to other people. We all do this! However, how are you supposed to find love again if you are not open to other possibilities? It is near impossible. Become conscious of this and, once you are somewhat ready (when are we *really* ready to get back into a relationship? Don't worry, I will tell you all about this later as well!), slowly reintegrate the dating scene. You may be surprised as to what there is out there for you.

➢ **You have unresolved problems with past relationships.** Are you still in love with you past partner? Do you think that there's a possibility for you two to get back together? If you have been in this relationship for a number of years, it may be hard for you to let go and move on, but it's important to do so to find love again. So, when you are wondering about why you have not been able to find love again in the past few months, take a deeper look at the potential feelings you may still have for your past partners. Now of course, if you have children or something along those lines (such as a dog), it may be difficult to completely cut them out of your life, but this is an exception. Otherwise, you should seriously attempt to cut out all problems in the past relationships you have had.

➢ **You have lost all hope in future love.** If you have been actively looking for love for a while now, it's possible that you have become discouraged and have the feeling that it'll never happen for you. This, however, is not true. Due to this, you may actually think it's worth it to settle for something that is only somewhat what you are looking for, just for the sake of having *someone*, but do not make this mistake as it is keeping you back from meeting someone that might actually be better for you. Now, don't take this as a cue to always break up relationships to find something better, as this is something we have talked about in the very first chapter.

If you resonate well with the latter three points, be conscious of this and decide what you want to do next. If you want to move on to find a great partner, follow the following steps outlined by the creators of the Law of Attraction.

Attracting the things you want

First, consciously make the decision that you want to look for love again and outline the traits you are looking for in a partner. In other words, design your perfect partner. Ask yourself the following; what are five to ten traits that you would love in a partner? Maybe categorize these into "must-haves", "would be great", and "that would be a plus''. Then, think about these traits from a different perspective; what traits in a partner would bring the best out of you? Once you have decided this, ask yourself how you would want to be treated by a potential partner, and what traits would be absolute no-gos. For example, the traits I would love in a partner are some such as ambition, dedication and passion. I also think that these traits would bring the best out of me, as someone who is passionate and ambitious brings out those same qualities in me; what makes a better team than one in which the players are extremely motivated to succeed or to achieve their goals?

This is the part about traits and about the other person. Let's take a deeper look at your personal wishes. What would you say is (or are) your biggest passion(s) in life? Is this so important that it would be unacceptable if a partner either did not share that passion, or did not support you with this? For example, if you wake up everyday and feel passionate about going to work, knowing that you will have a very long work day, do you think you would match well with somebody that does not like this? For example, I had a girlfriend once that was all about watching series. Of course, it would be great to watch some series once in a while together, but when I mean she was all about it, I mean, she was *all about it.* She would watch easily five or six hours of TV per day, and she loved it, but it drove me crazy after just a few months. When the newest season of Game of Thrones would come out, I would instantly know that I would be the one doing the dishes, cleaning up, doing the groceries and so on until she was done with it. Sure, she had a blog on which she was writing series critiques and was passionate about that, but it came to a point that I simply had nothing to talk to her about anymore. My experiences at work were not that interesting to her, and we began facing real problems. Where I loved going to work and achieving my entire to-do list, she despised the idea of having one at all. Thus, her passion and mine simply did not work well together. I am sure she also was completely turned off by my love of work; she did not understand it and would often tell me about capitalism and that my love for work was an illusion... Needless to say, we did not last very long. Ultimately, this little story serves to show you the importance of sharing a passion with someone, or, at the very least, to support and understand the other's passion.

Now very clear about the importance of fitting passions, think about what you consider is your life mission. What role would a partner play in this, and can they help you achieve this goal? An even more important question: do you want their help in this? For example, if your life mission is to help those in dire need in other countries, could your partner help you with this, and would you like them to? Some of us prefer having completely different lives than our partners', however, some of us also prefer sharing our activities, jobs and passions with them. Thus, in this case, maybe your perfect girlfriend or wife would want to become your business partner in a new Non-Governmental Organisation, for example. This is entirely up to you, but think about it as it will help you become clearer about the kind of person you would like to share your life with.

The next step is to look at yourself: become the person you want to have. Of course, this is not to be taken literally, but adopt the traits you want in someone else. If you want a partner that is spontaneous and outgoing, but that still has set life goals and a passion for this, make sure it is something you also offer. Otherwise, it will be very difficult to find someone with these traits that is willing to be in a partnership with someone with very different ones. Challenge yourself and your beliefs, and make space to grow as a person. You can become more of something by asking someone you know how they do it. For example, if your best friend is very spontaneous and this is a trait you would like to adopt, ask her how he does it; maybe he makes sure to leave himself enough time and space to take on other people's offers? Or, maybe he simply does not plan out his days? The important factor to keep in mind here is that if you are looking for someone spontaneous, the likelihood is that this partner will probably not be interested if you are unable to be spontaneous, simply because a match between a spontaneous person and someone that must plan out activities weeks in advance is bound to have some problems in the long-run.

The final step in this is to put yourself out there– no one can know that you're available if you do not make this clear. Additionally, make it clear for yourself, and this is where positive affirmations come in. Write down what you are manifesting, and say it out loud, for example "I am ready for love and welcome my soulmate in my life". It may sound ridiculous at first, but countless people have done this, and it has worked for them. Why not give it a try? The worst thing that can happen is it not working. As we've discussed in the previous chapter, confidence in yourself as a person is important, and so is confidence in your convictions. Confidence in what you say and in your belief that you *can and will find this person* is just as important. Believing in this is a vital step towards a healthy, happy and fulfilling relationship!

Following these steps, you are ready to attract people with a similar vibe, or at least a similar mindset when it comes to the kind of partner each is looking for. Of course, dating takes a lot of work and is demanding; no one is born perfect, and we all have something to work on one way or another. Now equipped with the basics of the Law of Attraction and some insights on dating, let's look into the concrete information: where to find love, how to approach others, and being careful with dating, as it's quite a dangerous world out there! Finding love can be done in many places, including apps, at work, or in social events. So, let's take a deeper look at this.

Chapter Four

Where Do I Find Love?

We've talked about the history of dating, the importance of being happy with yourself before starting a relationship, and about the law of attraction. Now, it's time to start looking at things more concretely: where can you find love? You are in luck, we now live in a society with more people than ever, and on top of this, in a world in which one can travel around quite a bit! So, you are not forced to stay in one place and you can find love, or a potential partner, anywhere. Now of course, finding a potential partner while traveling may not be the best case scenario, especially if this person lives across the planet, but it is a possibility. Who says you have to find someone that lives close to you?

In this chapter, I will give you my top tips on where, concretely speaking, you can find love. As I have had quite a bit of experience with dating men in my life, without trying to sound like I know it all, I think I am the right person to give you some insight on this. You see, my past boyfriends all came from different places. One was originally from Ghana, another from Russia, and my most recent ex-boyfriend and I got together in Morocco. Now, I would be lying if I said that long-distance is easy, but it is doable! So, this is the first tip I want to give you: open yourself up to the world and go on a trip. If you are able to, book yourself hostels, or sign up for free walking tours to meet new people. If you have the means to do it, and if you are able to take some time off from work, consider going on a longer trip with a specific group, as this is what I did and I was able to find love through this. Indeed, when you spend a few months with the same group of people, especially a group of people that each have very similar passions in life as you do (for example, traveling), you can easily find somebody that you get along with very well. So, why not check out your options in this regard? Maybe you have been slightly bored lately, or maybe you are ready for a new adventure? Then why not start traveling around? By visiting new places, meeting new people and experiencing different cultures, you also enrich yourself as a person, so give it a go!

Your community

Now, if traveling is not a possibility for you, that's okay. I understand that many of us have responsibilities, commitments that keep us where we are. If this is your case, do not feel doomed– there are many other options for you. For example, start looking in your own community. With this, I am not saying to look at all of your friends and debate which one to date next– this is bound to go horribly wrong!–, but, think about the parties you can attend, the events you can go to, and thus, who you could potentially meet there. I think one of the main mistakes many of us make at an older age is to stay home when we should be out socializing. 'I'm tired', 'I've had a long week'– all things that I can understand, but you want to find love, right? You won't find it in the comfort of your sofa. Well, unless you stick to online dating, but more on that later.

So, as I said, start looking in your own community. Ask around about parties and events, and try to attend a few every month or so. In the same line of ideas, look online at websites like MeetUp, which are great to get to know new people. This website is one on which different activities and meetups are listed, thus you can go to a few events depending on what you are passionate about. For example, if you really like walking around lakes and longing rivers, there are groups for this. Or, if you thoroughly enjoy trying different types of wines and cheeses, find a meetup along those lines and attend it. It is somewhat scary to put oneself out there and to go to a meetup full of people we don't know, but that's the beauty of it: no one knows you. So, if you do something you regret, you can always choose to never go again! What's the worst that can happen?

Similarly, if you would really love to try out wines and cheeses, but there is no meetup for it, simply start one! This is why such websites are great, anybody can create a meetup, so you do not have to attend a conference on a topic you have no interest in simply for the sake of meeting someone new. Be proactive, start an activity and make others join you.

I have also found that team sports are really wonderful at creating connections. For example, back when I used to play basketball, I loved playing with different members and being pushed to my limits; there's something empowering about it. Sports are something that we can all connect to quite well, and it is usually very intense. Aside from being very healthy, and a boost in your confidence (do you recall what we discussed in the second chapter?), it creates a feeling of belonging with others. Knowing that on Tuesdays at 7 PM you are meeting the team is exciting! And, on top of this, by meeting new people and creating a new circle of friends, you are increasing your chances of finding someone you can fall in love with. For example, if Martin from football practice invites you to a get together his best friend is planning on Friday, who knows who else will be there? This is a great way to expand your friend circle, and this way to also start meeting people that have similar passions and interests as you.

The complex debate of dating at the workplace

Now, let's talk about a place to meet others that could lead to problems: your workplace. I know that you may find Rebecca or Natalie very sweet and potentially attractive, but what is the etiquette on work-related relationships? It makes a lot of sense: we spend numerous hours in the same office with the same people. We create relationships with them, inside jokes, and take our breaks together. So, it's normal to think that feelings may develop over time, especially due to the amount of time spent together. But, is this actually allowed, or is it even ethical?

Well, first of all, this depends greatly on the rules set out by your employer, so get your contract out and check if there's anything in it on that topic. I have had employers in the past include specific rules and regulations to stick by, and dating coworkers was a reason to get fired, so do not let your love-seeking be the reason you are back on the job market looking for employment. Now, if your contract does not mention anything about colleagues dating each other, think about it deeply. If you find yourself sort of falling for someone, keep the following in mind: once the relationship goes south, you still have to come in to work and see them every day. So, your decision will depend quite a bit on how hard you fall, and how easy it is for you to get back up. For example, I know friends of mine who take a week to get over a breakup, but I also know others that cannot see their ex girlfriend in the first few months without being emotionally destroyed. So, think about your past relationship history. How did your previous relationships end? Are you still friends with your exes, and if so, how long did it take for it to be this way; did you need a few months without any contact? If you need a few months, you may want to avoid a workplace relationship as it may affect your career in the end. This being said, if you are a young adult working a part-time job as a waiter simply working there for the summer, then these questions may be slightly irrelevant for you! On the other hand, if you work a full-time office job and know this is the job you want to do for the next few years, seriously consider the impact a relationship could have on this. I know, falling for someone is irrational, but you have to think rationally about this! And of course, the relationship may be great, but you cannot ignore the risks that come with it, especially if it impacts your work and career opportunities.

Now setting some of this negative thinking aside, let's say that you have no problem getting over someone and that you know it would not be difficult for you to face Mary the day after being dumped (or dumping...). What is Mary's dating experience? Has she dated anyone in the office before, and if so, what was the outcome of this? If you think this is appropriate, you can discuss this openly with her, and share your fears with her on this. If Mary is known as someone who falls in love quickly and who stays in love for a long time post-break-up, keep this in mind for the same reasons mentioned above. Think about how compatible you really are and try hanging out outside of the office more often. You may realise that, in fact, you do not have much in common outside of work! And, this leads to problems.

An important factor of workplace relationships is the hierarchy: is this person your superior? Or, are you in charge of them? In the best case scenario, are you at the same stage of the hierarchy? This is vital to think about! You do not want to come home to a fight because you were asked to get coffee for the team, or because you spoke to your partner, who at work is your employee, in a way they did not like it. For example, when I was much younger, I used to work for an ice cream shop. Although I did not work with a boyfriend, I got my best friend hired and became her superior. Let me just say that she quit soon enough as she could not handle being under me in the hierarchy– it would seriously bother her to have to do what I told her to do, and this is only in an ice cream shop! Mix this with wanting to feel loved and wanting support from your lover, and this is where things can go seriously wrong. This is where I warn you: you have to be very sure about your capacity to deal with a difference in ranking. Because of this, I would sincerely advise you against dating your boss, especially if you are at the beginning of your career. Think about it, if this relationship goes wrong, are you going to be able to get references from your employer? Will you be able to get promoted, or will there always be a feeling of 'they got this promotion because they're sleeping with the boss' in the air at the office? I know, you can't help who you love, but just make sure to be aware of this! If you find yourself getting feelings for someone that you find would be a bad idea to date, I suggest you stop yourself right away. If you think it is appropriate, you can let this person know in advance, simply by telling them "I think we need to put some space between each other", and the likelihood is that they will know what the reason for this is. It's hard, but it's worth it, as you do not want to jeopardize your career prospects over a love affair that may not be worth it.

This all being said, it is also possible to find love at work. I know this might sound quite counter-intuitive considering the past chapters, but hear me out. Work is the place you most likely spend the most time excluding your bed, so it can be tough to think that this is not a potential place for love, right? Well, if you decide to give it a shot, it can work out! I would simply advise you to make clear 'rules'

Approaching women in public

So now you may wonder, if you cannot date someone at work, the place where you probably spend the most time, where else? Well as mentioned in the first part of this chapter, you can look at clubs, sports, and parties through common friends. However if this does not work, you can also try something unconventional nowadays: approaching people in public. Shocking, I know! In this day and age, it has become quite a *weird thing* to go up to people to date, however just a few decades ago, this was one of the only ways! So let's brainstorm the number of places one can meet others, and let's talk about when it's appropriate, and when you should avoid it.

First, the places. I know life is not a romantic movie like The Notebook or Dear John, but, this does not mean that you cannot take the tactics they use in such movies. My tip: aim for public places where your potential date feels comfortable. For example, if you go to a coffee shop and see a woman reading one of your favourite books, you can write her a quick note mentioning this! For example:

Hey, I'm Jonah. I see that you're reading X book, and it's one of my favourites! I didn't want to disturb your reading, but, how do you feel about meeting sometime to talk about it together?

Let me know,
+1 234 567 8901
Jonah

This is the way to do it if you're unsure about bothering someone. This way, you are respecting the other person's space, meanwhile you're also taking the chance. And, what's the worse that can happen? You won't receive a call or text, that's it!

Apart from coffee shops, you can meet people practically anywhere. At the beach, at the movies while in line, in a bar... However if you are not feeling too confident about going on your own, ask a few of your friends to go with you! And, a top tip from me: go with a few girls as well, who can help you out by playing the wing-man. You see, women usually feel more comfortable speaking to men when there are other women around, there's a feeling of safety and it's more comfortable! So ask your best girl friends to come with you and let them approach these women for you. I have had a girl come up to me in a bar and tell me 'my friend thinks you're cute! If you want, I can introduce you guys…', and this guy turned out to be really great. Try it out!

This being said, some of us are quite shy. And if this is your case, then you were born in the perfect era. Nowadays, you do not need to go outside of your house to try dating, although this tends to work pretty well. Indeed, you can now simply use apps, such as Happn, Tinder, OkCupid or Bumble if you want to let women write you instead of always having to make the first step. So, let's look at each of these in more detail.

What about online dating?

Happn is a dating app which is relatively new. It is based on the idea that we constantly run into people that we may find attractive, but which we may not have the guts to go speak to. Thus, it looks at your location and suggests to you the people that you may have run into that day. This app tends to be helpful to find others, however, unfortunately as we tend to go to the same places, the same twenty or so people keep popping up, limiting the number of dates you may be able to make.

Tinder, on the other hand, works differently. If you do not know this app yet, it is one that you can use to find the different potential matches around you. In simple terms, this app can be tweaked to find women in a certain age and mile or kilometer range. Thus, you get to choose which kinds of women you would like to be matched with– perhaps you get along well with women your age or somewhat older, and perhaps you would prefer not having to travel ten or fifteen kilometers to meet this person (this is mostly for my European readers!). On Tinder, you simply have to swipe left or right depending on how you find this person. You can write a short biography and can include what you do for a living. This being said, Tinder is known as an app that is primarily used for hookups. You can try to mention that you are looking for something more serious, but many women on there are also looking for something casual.

OkCupid, on the other hand, is an app and a dating website that offers you a better chance of finding someone that actually is looking for something serious. Unlike Tinder, OkCupid requires you to answer a few questions and to describe who you are, what you are looking for, and so on in more detail. Thus, the users are most often looking for something serious, as someone only looking for hookups and so on is less likely to actually take the time to create an elaborate profile. My tip: use this website to find people with whom you have a lot more in common. You can actually choose what you are looking for, and the website will suggest people based on this, and based on your other answers by using an algorithm that matches your answers and gives you a percentage– for example, you are 95% a match with this person.

Apart from Tinder, another app that is growing in popularity is Bumble. This one works similarly; you match someone by going through their pictures and reading through their biography text. However, Bumble is different as the lady is in charge of texting the man first, thus taking out the stress that comes with finding a good pick up line, and the disappointment that comes with never getting answers from women. I know, it's awful that we tend not to answer, but honestly speaking, sometimes life just works in a way that one simply cannot answer or does not have the time for it. Thus, with this app, the woman has 24 hours to write, otherwise the match gets deleted. If you are somewhat shy, this app may be the right one for you.

There are numerous other apps available out there for you if you find these to be disappointing. And, of course, you can choose to stay away from them, but they really do make life easier sometimes, especially if you do not have the time or energy to attend numerous social events to meet people in real life. Ultimately, you have various options as to where to meet women. If you prefer doing this in real life, you can opt for coffee shops or bars, but my best tip would be to stick to friend groups and to try going to more social events with them. As I told you, going with a larger group and approaching women this way is usually more successful, at least from my perspective, it's easier to make a connection with someone this way as it feels safer, and more like making new friends than going straight into flirting. This being said, this brings up a few questions, namely how do you approach a woman? I already gave you a quick example a few pages ago, but let's go more in depth, as this is usually where things go wrong; one says the wrong thing, or approaches a woman at the wrong time... How do you avoid this? This is what I will discuss in the following chapter, so keep on reading!

Chapter Five

Approaching Others

Over the course of the previous chapter, we looked at the different places you could potentially find love. From the workplace to bars and other public places, there are numerous situations and areas you could find somebody. This being said, we have not yet addressed the more complex parts of dating: approaching others in a flirting context. Dating is exciting and nerve-wracking, and saying the right thing at the right moment can be a game changer. On the other hand, saying the wrong thing can also ruin all of your efforts. So, in this chapter, I will be giving you tips on how to approach a woman in order to sweep her off of her feet. As always, this is from my perspective, so you can trust that I really know what I am talking about. There is a fine line between trying to be sweet and nice to a woman and coming off as creepy, which, as I am sure you can imagine, is something you should definitely avoid.

Is your shyness hindering you from potential dates?

Before going into depth about how to approach a woman, let's speak about a factor that tends to impact many men and the way they approach others: shyness. Indeed, being shy is something tough to work with, especially when it comes to going up to a stranger. It's understandable that you may be shy when trying to flirt; ultimately, you are showing somebody that you like them, perhaps based on their attitude or their looks, and you are putting yourself up to the possibility that this person may very well reject you, and rejection is hard on the ego! So just how can you put this shyness away to have a successful conversation with a woman? In all honesty, one of my best tips is simply to fake it until you make it. You may be very shy, but one of the most attractive traits on a man tends to be confidence; knowing what he wants. So, remember the second chapter where I gave you tips on improving your confidence? Go read it again if you need to, but as I said confidence takes time to build. Thus, fake the confidence until you really possess it!

A great way to get pastpast shyness is to keep in mind the worst case scenario. For example, before going up to a woman, ask yourself what is the worst thing that can happen.

Sure, if she rejects you it may hurt your ego a little bit, but what if you never try? In the same line of ideas, someone can hardly remember you if you were in a group setting and did not say anything. So even just starting by having some small talk, asking her how her weekend was and what she's been up to is a great way to start a conversation. On top of this, this way you can start realizing that this person is, in fact, just another person. She is simply another woman living on this planet, so, there's no need to feel so shy or embarrassed. The main thing to keep in mind is that being shy is something you can change. You can take steps to become more confident, and can slowly work on speaking to more people openly without feeling flushed every time. Again, this is all rooted in confidence!

You see, I used to be very shy myself. Although it was not necessarily related to dating, I would have a very hard time going up to people in conferences and introducing myself as I was extremely self-conscious. Although the people that were there were incredible and seemed very nice and open-minded, the minute that the time came to go up to them and introduce myself, I would be overwhelmed and would forget the things I wanted to ask them, so I would just back away and let others go up to them instead. Needless to say, this is something that held me back many years, especially because these people could have been great in terms of career opportunities. I still regret being this way today! So you may wonder, how did I change the way I act around others? Well, I worked on my confidence using the tips I outlined in the second chapter and began thinking much more rationally. I would ask myself 'what do I have to lose? What is the worst that can come out of this situation? Maybe this person will not like me, or maybe they will think that I am absolutely clueless, but at least I will have introduced myself!', and this was a game changer. I began seeing things from a new perspective: every opportunity that is not taken is an opportunity wasted. Although my example is not related to dating directly, it is absolutely applicable to your situation if you, like me, suffer from the shyness syndrome. So the next time that you spot this person at work, in a bar or at a sports club, do not let it overcome you and be rational about it. What's the worse that can happen?

How *not* to approach a woman

If you're not shy, lucky you! However, you also have some things to watch out for when approaching women, other than the time and place you are doing so. So, let's think about the different situations possible and how to act in each. First, how should you make the first move? Should you even make it, or should you let the woman make it? Now this is going to be controversial, especially with the new debates brought up by feminism, but women do like being approached first! Sure, some will make the first move and some even prefer it this way, but I think I speak for numerous women when I say that there is something great about being approached by a man that shows interest. So, my first tip is to be friendly— I know, this one sounds obvious. But really, be friendly. Too many women tend to be approached by men in social events where they end up feeling like a prize to show off in front of friends, especially when we see that the group of ten other guys behind them is chuckling and acting foolishly. So, be kind and nice, while showing confidence. If your friends are indeed chuckling in the background, maybe apologize and explain that you've been contemplating the different ways you can make your move, so they are simply watching the outcome! This sounds quite cute and it is definitely enticing.

Additionally, while you approach a woman, try your very best to keep your smile on, and your phone away. There is nothing more annoying than a guy that is interrupted by fifteen WhatsApp notifications, and honestly, it only makes us wonder who it is that you're talking to (*am I the fifth girl you're trying this with today??*). Smile often, ask questions, and show real interest! For example, ask her questions about what she does for a living, what she is doing at this exact location, and if she's enjoying herself. Granted, not all women are the same, and depending on where you are meeting this woman, her expectations may be different from yours, or vice versa!

Meeting someone face-to-face is different from online dating, so this is what we are covering first, but do not worry, we will also cover online dating shortly.

When it comes to the kinds of conversations you are having and the way you speak, there are a few things that tend to be turn-offs for women, namely things such as arrogance and a know-it-all attitude. The tricky thing here is that while confidence is attractive, it can easily turn to arrogance if you go over the top with it. Therefore, keep this in mind. Instead of saying something along the lines of *"I was so good at football that my coach bribed me to stay!"*, aim for something more like *"I got really lucky because my coach insisted that I stay, I guess he really values me and that's awesome!"*, which, instead of focusing on you and showing how amazingly great you are, focuses on the fact that you are humble enough to mention that you were *lucky*. This is a really important point, so make sure to keep it in mind as a slip of the tongue can completely turn off your potential date.

When you flirt, however, don't set aside showing off completely. Sharing your achievements and things you are proud of is great, actually, as women look for men that have impressive things to offer. However, you can make sure not to come off as arrogant by taming it down a bit with a humorous tone. For example:

"Yeah, I actually received the Most Valuable Player award for football. I really think I should change my last name to Neuer, actually, we're basically the same now!"

This is funny, light-hearted and will definitely earn you some laughter! And humor is always a great thing to have.

While humor is wonderful, be careful about the jokes you make. Some jokes are funny, but no one likes being made fun of, even if it is meant in a cute, flirty way. And I speak from experience! I actually had a horrible two-day long date a year ago. You see, I had met this person online through a chat (I know what you're thinking... what good can come out of this? Just wait!). We had been talking for over two months, and we lived approximately a 6-hour train ride away. So, when the right time came, I invited him to come visit me—a mistake. I actually invited him to stay at my place since he was on a tight budget (yes, mistake number two!). When he arrived, I was shocked to realize that he was a completely different person than who he claimed to be. The man I had been speaking to was long gone, and he made place for someone sarcastic and plain rude. I did not quite understand why this was happening as on the phone and video calls he was sweet, but the minute we met, he showed me what I guess is his real self. I still remember when we went for coffee, and we were inside the very tiny shop. We were in line and there was barely any space to stand, so I asked him if he wanted anything as I was inviting him, and he said no, so I told him maybe he could wait outside because there was absolutely no space. To this, he screamed "FINE! I GET IT! YOU DON'T WANT TO HANG OUT WITH ME!", which, although was (hopefully) meant in a teasing, funny way, made me look insane. I did not know how to react, so I laughed it off, but the woman next to me seemed completely gobsmacked and asked me if I was okay— I was, but I just had no idea how to handle the situation. I paid and went outside to meet him, and while we sat down, he 'jokingly' pushed me aside a bit, making me drop my coffee on myself which not only hurt quite a bit but again left me speechless. He laughed it off and did not seem to realize that this wasn't flirting, it was just rude.

You see, after this 'date' (I don't even know if I can call it a date...), we went back to my place and I told him I needed to do something just to get away from him for an hour. He left the next day and sent me a message saying thank you, that he had loved his weekend. To this day, I still have absolutely no idea what was going on in his mind. Needless to say, that was the end of that!

What I hope you can get from this short story is that what you may think comes off as funny or playful can be hurtful or simply a complete turn off for someone. Of course, my example was quite extreme! However, the fact that the guy never realized that his way of treating me was completely out of bounds is an example of how you may be doing something with good intentions, for example trying to connect with the woman you are speaking to by teasing her, which would ultimately be received in a terrible way. So, to make sure that you aren't overstepping, maybe start by saying a few jokes, being a tad sarcastic, and try to see how the other person reacts. All women are different and some will take sarcasm and irony better than others, but play it safe.

When should I message her? How often?

One of the problems I hear about quite often from male friends of mine is that the women they speak to suddenly stop answering, or show less interest after they send a specific message. On my part, while I date there are specific things I will automatically stop responding to. For example, when I am writing with a man I have never met before, such as someone I have met on Tinder, if the person brings on something about sex or even just jokes about it, it is an instant turn off. Sure, maybe in the long-run I would be interested, but bringing the subject up before we have even met is a clear sign to me that this person is interested in one thing and this one thing only. If this is not the case, then it is their mistake as this is the message that is being sent across— and this is not only me, ask your female friends, I can guarantee you they will say the same. Similarly, if a guy puts too much pressure to meet before we've had a conversation over a few days (for example : *I don't want to wait to meet you, you're so incredibly interesting! Let's meet tomorrow. Oh, you can't? Then the day after. Or the day after that. Or now. Can you meet now?*). This sends two messages; first, the man has nothing else to do, which isn't very attractive as someone that is busy and that has an active lifestyle is great. After all, a relationship should not be all about spending every minute of every day with the same person, right? In my opinion, a person should *add* to your life, not over take it. But that might just be me. The second message this sends is that the person has some boundary issues, as it puts immense amounts of pressure on me to make time for this person right away as they just cannot wait. I know, this may sound somewhat rough to hear, but you bought this book to learn the best tricks to a healthy and functional relationship, right? Well, this is one of them: take your time, do not put too much pressure, and be ready to put some effort into it.

Ok, given, this is a situation that mostly occurs on dating websites and apps. Thus, let's look at dating online, and how to approach women on such platforms as this is drastically different from other forms of dating, namely offline. The way to approach women will depend on the app you use and what you are looking for. On apps such as Tinder, it is often expected that the people are mainly looking for sex. However, the biography section usually is a dead-giveaway. For example, if a woman says straight up that she is not looking for one night stands, then at least you know. However, if this is not clearly written, there are a few tricks you can use to find out smoothly that don't include asking "so what are you looking for on here" (which in itself is quite telling of your expectations!).

So, it's a match! The girl you like has matched you too and you're now at the stage of writing. Some will text first, but honestly speaking, this is still most often expected of the man. Why, you ask? Because often when women text first, men tend to unmatch. Now, I am not a man, so I am not the best person to tell you why this is the case, but I think it may have something to do with the chase. So why not just text first? The worst that can come out of it is either you get unmatched or you don't receive an answer.

Your first message should be witty, thoughtful and respectful. A great message can be a corny pickup line followed by a cute GIF, for example. Usually, this is the message I will answer first as it shows that the guy has taken the time to come up with something fun, or at least that they have humor in the instance that they send the same message to all women– which is fine too! Then, once the conversation is started, go into small talk, find out more about this woman; what she does for a living, what she does in her free time, what her favorite bar is, and so on. From this, you can start having an idea of what you guys could do on a date. Once the conversation is flowing, you're making her laugh, and she seems to be enjoying the conversation (which you can find out by the amount of text she uses to answer, how open or closed she is to your questions, and whether she also asks you questions or not), you can ask her out. She may ask you out first, so that's great! I would advise you to think of somewhere in public, such as in a park or over drinks; nothing too fancy. Although going for dinner used to be the to-go date, I find that, nowadays, drinks or coffee tends to be the better (and cheaper!) option for first dates. You could also invite her for a beer near a lake or river if you live in such an area, or something along those lines. Or, if you have something in common, such as gaming, you can also invite her for a gaming tournament (maybe online first?). The goal is to keep it in public to offer her some safety (remember what we talked about in the previous chapter?).

This goes well for an app like Tinder. On another app or website, such as OkCupid, you have more luck. This website aims at really presenting yourself and your passions or hobbies, so most often women's profiles will tell you a lot more than a picture and a small body of text on Tinder will. To impress her, check out her profile, find something that you think is interesting, and ask her more about it. Avoid the simple 'Hey' or 'How are you doing?', as I can guarantee you that they probably receive dozens of such messages every day, thus try to stand out by showing that you actually tried and were interested in her and what she has to say.

All in all, my tip is to avoid anything that comes off as too pushy or aggressive, such as the example I gave you earlier with the person putting pressure on the other to meet. If you can, avoid bringing up sex before meeting the person, and even then, I would wait until you feel completely comfortable about it. Some women are very open-minded about it, meanwhile others absolutely hate the idea of being asked about sex right away. This way, you can also avoid being creepy or seen as someone that only wants one thing. And yes, I know it may not be the nicest thing to hear, but slow down and don't expect too much right away! Slow down, if you show that you are busy and have things to do, in other words if you play somewhat hard to get, it is much more interesting than if you are ready and available at any time. Also, it gives you something to talk about once you do meet! Over the course of this chapter, hopefully you were able to have a better idea of how to approach women both in public and on dating apps. It's definitely tricky and which requires navigation, but at the very root, it's about being yourself and realizing that the right person will be there at the right time, so forcing things or trying to make things work with someone that seems uninterested isn't worth spending energy on, no matter how much you want it to happen!

By now, you should be ready to work on your confidence, should know how to meet women and where, and should be able to approach them in a way that is welcoming and successful. So, it's time to look into concrete things: the first dates, where to have them, how to prepare and how to succeed in them, and how to make sure to score a second date. Let's get into it!

Chapter Six

The First Date

By now, we have discussed how to approach women on different apps and in real-life. Now, it's time to explore the first date: where to go on a first date, how to get ready for it, what to be careful about, how and when to approach sex, and how to deal with rejection (or rejecting someone in a nice way!). Thus, throughout this chapter, we will look at each of these in detail. By the end of this part of the book, you should feel confident about suggesting a first-date idea to a woman and all that this entails. So, let's jump right into it: where should the first date take place?

Picking the location

In the previous chapter, I briefly mentioned that the first date should ideally take place somewhere in public, simply to avoid any awkward situation, or to avoid having to deal with rejecting someone in their own home. This usually puts one in a situation that is quite tough to handle, especially when it is completely out of one's comfort zone! So, why not try to find more neutral places to meet? For example, I would suggest that you go for something with quite a few people around. You can start by going on a walk with a coffee as walking past certain things may give you ideas as to what you could speak about, and, let's be honest, awkward silences are often one of the things we are worried about. I have always found that first dates should be easy to go along with– for example, some great dates are going to play light sports together (who wants to appear all sweaty?), or even simpler things like grabbing a drink or getting a coffee. If you grab a beer and live in a country where it's in fact legal to drink outside, I would suggest sitting down somewhere in a park and enjoying a simple conversation– it does not have to be complicated for the date to be great! And, no, you are not expected to take out hundreds of dollars to impress your date.

Although sitting in a park may be a good idea if you want to be able to fully concentrate on what your date is explaining, I certainly prefer active dates. In fact, I find it much better as it stimulates my mind. Instead of going to the movies, where you basically sit awkwardly while waiting for the other to grab your hand, or vice versa, why not go skating, hiking, or even just go to a small, local farmer's market? And, if the conversation runs short, you can always comment on how great the apples at the next stand look. Just to give you a few ideas, here is my list of favorite first dates:

1. Going   for   a   drink

   No, it's not because I like free wine. It's simple: it can be very uncomfortable to meet somebody that you have never met before, especially if the goal is to see if you are a potential match. In fact, both of you are trying to show the best versions of yourself, so a cocktail can relieve some of this tension. On top of this, I often found that once one starts to drink, a part of their true self shows. Sure, it can be a bit awkward at first, but once you both start taking a few sips, I can guarantee that you will start feeling a lot more comfortable. It always works for me, at least!

2. Going for a walk around the city– but this one works best with newcomers

Of course, you may not always meet people that have just moved to your city. But, I have met one or two that had just moved to mine, and it was always great to give them a free walking tour. I live in Germany, so during the winter, we even did a Christmas Market tour, where we walked over ten kilometers and had a 'Glühwein', or a hot wine, every couple of markets we would pass by– a nice way to warm up! If you live in a smaller village or rarely see newcomers, this may not be your best option. But, you could also be a 'tourist in your own city' and take this opportunity to go check out all the landmarks you have never visited. I find it's an amazing way to see something new while getting to know someone.

3. Visit your local zoo

Again, this one depends on the resources available to you. In my city, there is a zoo that can be visited almost all year-long, thus it's always quite nice. I never get tired of seeing wild animals, and, it is very difficult for a date to go badly in such a situation.

I have numerous more favorite ways to get to meet someone. As mentioned, getting a coffee, going for dinner, going to the beach, there are numerous options. This being said, I am certain that you are getting the point– go for something simple that can be distracting, this way you can feel more comfortable and can always find something to speak about. Now, let's talk about a crucial element: how to get ready for a date.

Dating 101

When I say 'get ready for a date', if your first reaction is 'there are steps to follow?', then I urge you to read this paragraph while paying close attention. In fact, it happens quite often that a very small mistake can completely ruin the efforts you have put into the rest of the dating process. So, let's talk about it. Of course, there are the basics such as making sure that your date is still in, and double checking that you are meeting at a certain place at a certain type. Once this is done, the real work begins.

It happens too many times when a date comes to the meeting point a few minutes too late. Going back to the example of the date I told you about in the previous chapter, on top of being very boring, this guy arrived over twenty minutes late. I was standing outside, in front of the restaurant, for quite a long time! It was quite cold and rainy, as it often does in my city, and I was checking my phone to make sure that he would show up. I can understand that sometimes things happen, but I found that it made for a pretty bad first impression!

During this date, something that annoyed me more was the fact that he never let me know how late he would be. When he arrived, he told me that his phone had died– and here's my next tip. Make sure that you have enough battery on your phone to reduce your stress. You might need your map app to find the place, or if you cannot find it or are going to be late, you want to be sure to be able to let your date know that you are running a few minutes late– but try to be on time.

Alongside this, make sure to bring some cash with you. Again, I live in Germany, where everything is based on cash. So, it has happened many times that I witnessed two people on a date, usually expats, who only had cards. It makes it so much more complicated– one has to go get money out, which can trigger a bit of a conflict on who pays, and so on. Talking about paying, what do you think is the etiquette regarding paying for a dinner? I believe that this depends on the generation, but, it also has a lot to do with age and context. For example, again using the bad date that I recently went on, we paid separately, most likely because we both realized that the date was going pretty terribly. However, on many dates, as the woman, I get invited. Personally, my rule is always 'I'll get it next time!', which both serves as a way to say 'I don't expect you to pay every time' and 'I would like to see you again'. However, if a woman offers to split or to pay the bill, unless you really want to insist, I would simply agree or suggest that she takes the next round. You can also joke about it a bit, just to break any tension that might build up.

Going back to the first impression, I would be lying to you if I said that women only look at your personality. In fact, you probably also judge according to looks as well. I encourage you to make sure that you dress in a way that makes you feel confident. On top of this, make sure that you look well-polished: so, take a nice shower, make sure your beard is well trimmed, your nails are clean, and so on. I know this may sound obvious to you, but it would seriously surprise you to hear about the horror stories many girls have had in regards to cleanliness and hygiene!

Additionally, you can make sure to choose your outfit the night before to avoid some stress. To choose it, why not ask your girlfriends (as in, friends that happen to be girls) to help you out? They probably have a good idea. My tips: find something that shows your best attributes, meanwhile, do not show up in sweats; you are not on your couch! However, make sure that the clothes you choose to wear are also comfortable as, hopefully, your date will go on long enough that you will want to be feeling comfortable! Also, make sure to use some cologne, that's a nice way to show your date that you put effort into your date.

Ultimately, if you follow these tips, you should have no problem making a great first impression. This being said, let's look into one of the issues that may come up once you are on the first date, or in the following ones: sex.

When to have it? How do I approach it? How do you know if the other really wants it? These are all the questions we ask ourselves, and, in my opinion, there is no right or wrong answer as everyone is different, but there are a few certain things that you should be careful about in terms of how you show your interest to women.

My only tips regarding this is to follow your gut feeling, to make sure that you follow the flow, to not try too hard too quickly, and to learn to read signals. For example, if you have been on a date or two with a girl, and she is clearly flirting with you and getting closer physically to you, you can offer to take this back to your place. If she says no, make sure to show her that this is okay, as insisting is only annoying and will push her away– trust me! There is really nothing worse than having to tell someone 'no' in a nice way multiple times, just to realize that they won't get the hint. Believe me on this; once, when a date came to an end and I needed to go home as it was a work night and I needed to be up early the next day, I told my date that I needed to get some sleep. He asked if I wanted to stay at his, and I explained that I needed to go to work the next day, so that it would not be professional to arrive there looking like a mess. His answer was ' well that's okay, but only if you're not using this as an excuse!', and let me tell you, I instantly lost all attraction for this guy. I know, you may think I made a huge deal out of nothing, but the reality is that no girl likes to feel like we owe someone something, or like we are only allowed to say no if we have a valid excuse– if we don't want to, that's the end of the story, and the same is true for you too! So keep this in mind: you are much more likely to have success in your quest for sex if you respect the woman's boundaries.

Regarding the number of dates, or how to know when is the right time, in my opinion, there is no specific number of dates that makes it right. For some, they will want to do it right away, while others prefer waiting a significant amount of time. To figure this out, if your date is not showing any signs or even mentioning something about it, you could take the first step and allude to it after a few dates. Do not be too invasive about it, maybe just invite her over in order to cook her something, and see if anything happens. If it does not, or if she shows little interest, maybe you can ask her via text later on. Now, you may wonder why via text– remember what I mentioned about asking a girl out while you are in public, and avoiding doing so while you are in a situation that she could perceive as dangerous? This is similar– asking her about sex while you are cooking for her, in your apartment, may send her the message that you have expectations, and she may fear your reaction if she rejects you, thus I suggest that you bring this up while there is somewhat of a separation between the two of you.

Dealing with rejection

Speaking of this, how do you deal with rejection? Hopefully, by using the tips and tricks I am sharing with you throughout this entire book, you will be able to navigate the dating scene in order to find yourself a great partner, nevertheless, rejection is always something that can occur! And it happens to everyone, to women as well. I can assure you that almost every single person on this planet has been rejected, perhaps with the exception of Victoria's Secret models. Us normal folks, however, get rejected quite often. So how do you deal with this? When I get rejected, the first thing I keep in mind is that I will not be everybody's cup of tea. I know it may sound cliché to you, but it's true: it's almost impossible to be attractive to every single person on this planet, whether this is in terms of looks or in terms of personality. You may have the best mustache, or the nicest laugh, but someone, somewhere in the world is bound to be annoyed by it or is probably going to strongly dislike it, it's the hard truth. So, knowing this, the second that you become able to accept this and that you can deal with it without letting it throw you off completely, the easier it will be to move on.

On top of this, I have found that having confidence in yourself and what you do is vital to make sure that rejection does not completely beat you down. I've spoken a lot about my younger years, and that's because these were very rough for my ego! As you know, I had very little confidence, so rejection would always throw me down even more. Nowadays, however, as I love my job, I run a business successfully, and am generally genuinely happy with the person I am, it has become much easier to accept rejection. I detach myself from the situation— this person does not like that one specific thing about me? That's okay, then that's just how things are. Try to care less about the things that you cannot change— and before you say you could change the other's mind, I am quite certain that if you were to try to do so, the other would simply get more annoyed. Just leave it alone, understand that it's not you as a person who is wrong, it's simply a component of your personality that may not be very compatible with the other person's.

Nevertheless, rejection hurts, I am not going to downplay it. As much as I can rationalize things, it still hurts at least a little bit to realize that somebody is not into you as much as you are into them. You may ask yourself why and think of where you went wrong, but from personal experience, it is better to leave it alone and to simply take for granted that the other person would prefer to have their space. Asking others what you did wrong, or why they're not interested, is most likely just going to confirm why they rejected you, thus I encourage you to stay away from this. Be the bigger person and choose to move on with your life– this one seems not to be right, so do not waste your time. Of course there are a few occasions, especially in American movies like The Notebook and The Last Song, where this can be different, but these are rare, so really try to gauge how much space you have to negotiate or to try to show the other that you may be more than what they think! All in all, I feel it is healthier to just move on rather than to try to force something to happen when one of the two seems less interested. This means, make an active choice to delete the person from your social media, and stop posting Instagram stories or Facebook statuses with the hope that the person sees *how great you are and how much they are missing out on*– I'm only saying this because it's something I've done and that I am not proud of!

Rejecting others respectfully

If you have been going out with somebody for a few weeks, but slowly find yourself feeling that you just aren't connecting as well as you used to or that you are losing interest, I would encourage you to let them know as soon as you can and to avoid leading them on. The later you do it, the more you will confuse the person and the more angry they will be with you, with good reason! However, there are ways to reject others that are nice and which do not feel like you are completely shattering their heart. Keep in mind that these people have feelings, potentially even some for you, and therefore respect this.

I would suggest that you take a moment to think about what you will tell them. Avoid only coming to a meetup and telling them that it is over, or even worse, ghosting them (a new term that refers to the process by which one simply stops answering calls and messages, meanwhile leaving the other utterly confused!). If you have been seeing someone, the minimum amount of respect you should have for this person, in my opinion, should be to let them know that you do not see yourself as a good fit for them. On top of this, I think the best way to do so is to let them know face-to-face, but this may differ depending on how long you have been seeing each other. For example, if you have been going on a few dates and are regularly texting, then it is important, in my opinion, that you respect this person by showing them appreciation and letting them know face to face that you think this is not working. However, if you only went on a date or two, I find that a simple text suffices.

If you do meet the person, I would suggest that you prepare yourself extensively, that you arrive at the meeting prepared to give them a reason, and that you are respectful of their feelings by taking your time to explain yourself. I would avoid going straight to it, but would first enjoy whatever you two are deciding to do, without avoiding it for too long. You may be thinking "I don't owe anyone an explanation!" and you are right, but human beings like to know where they went wrong, or what steps in the equation did not work well. Even if you just do not connect with the person, explaining that you feel they are not the greatest match can be a good way to let them know that it is not their fault, but really, that it *is* you! Stay honest and do not make up stories just to comfort them, but keep their feelings in mind. On top of this, I would seriously avoid using an accusatory tone– if you are cutting things off because of something they have done, saying "I cannot do this" is better than "you did this and I don't like that", as it's much harder to speak out against.

Once you have rejected the person, it is important that you give them some space. If they text you with the aim of figuring out what they did wrong or how they can change things, attempt to dissipate the tension by explaining that you have mentioned what you needed to mention, and that you will be moving on from now on. Do not fuel the pain they are feeling, simply take some distance.

Ultimately, they may not be able to take the hint. Thus, if you have tried to explain it to them nicely, you may need to be more to-the-point and less conscious of their feelings. If trying to be nice about it has not worked, keep it short and simple: "sorry, I am not interested and have explained this to you. I wish you all the best." and cut the conversation short. If they simply won't understand and won't leave you alone without a reason, using a small lie is not all that bad in this case. Making up that you are too busy at the moment, or that you are still in love with your ex, is possibly not the most ethical thing to do, but if you are facing somebody that just will not take no for an answer, you need to do what you need to do! Ultimately, put yourself first.

By now, we have closely looked at a few components of dating that tend to be tricky, such as finding the right date spot, getting ready for this date, and dealing with rejection, whichever side you may be on. I have said it many times and will continue saying it: dating is difficult! It takes a lot of work and can be emotionally exhausting, but following the outlined tips in this chapter, you should now be ready for a good first date, should know how to approach sex further down the lines, and should understand how to deal with rejection and how to reject someone if things don't turn out too great. In any case, we are slowly coming to the end of this book. Next up, we will be moving towards being happily single after a relationship, as they do not always end well, unfortunately. Thus, without further ado, let's get into the concluding chapter.

Chapter Seven

What If It's Over?

So far, we have talked about dating and confidence in a lot of depth, nevertheless, not all relationships last a lifetime. Indeed, some relationships are meant to be, meanwhile, others are bound to fail, unfortunately. Therefore, this book would not be complete without at least a chapter discussing how to get back up once one is broken up with, and how to be happily single *again*. We have already talked about boosting your confidence in order to be happily single while looking for love, but what about being happy again post break-up? Additionally, how can you notice when it is time to call the relationship off? Is there ever a good time to break things off, or is there a good way to do so in order to spare the other person's feelings? And, finally, how can you accept being broken up *with* without letting it get to you and break down the confidence you have worked so hard for? Over the course of this concluding chapter, we will take a look at each of these in depth, to finally be able to ensure that you are fully set, completely ready to enter the dating scene with fewer worries and a better confidence in regard to your potential successes!

Is it time to call it off?

First, let's discuss how to know whether it's time to leave the relationship or not. Usually, when you start thinking about leaving a relationship, or even just wonder if it is really working out the way you want it to, it is a pretty good indication that it may be time to seriously take the time to look at the pros and cons of your relationships. However, deciding to call off a relationship is dependent on a few more factors than just thinking about it once or twice; naturally, you will not have the same thought process if the person you are ending a relationship with is your wife of ten years versus a woman you have just started seeing a few months ago. There are various degrees of seriousness to a relationship that impact how you think it may work or not.

To give you an example, while I was abroad on a trip to Algeria, I met a nice young man that I really connected well with. I spent a total of two months there, and we started having feelings for each other towards the end of the first month. If you know a bit about Algeria or other North African countries and/or the Middle Eastern culture, you will know that dating is not as simple to them as it is to those in the West in many cases. Usually, dating is meant to go somewhere towards marriage, and children are almost always a must. As I was quite young when I met this man and was just beginning my career, I was not ready for a serious relationship in terms of getting married and having children, and, on top of this, I had to leave after a few weeks of being with him. It is very difficult for Algerians to receive visas, thus, this made our relationship almost impossible, even in terms of long-distance– I simply could not imagine being in a long distance relationship with a man I had been seeing for two months who had very different expectations from mine. However, once I left, I found it extremely difficult to end the relationship as it also meant that my trip was over, that this part of my life would never happen again, thus it was very heartbreaking. In any case, breaking up was extremely tough, but it was necessary for me to regain joy and happiness, especially since I felt trapped once back at home and still in a relationship, technically, with this man. Nevertheless, breaking up gave me my freedom again– I was able to continue concentrating on my career, and he was able to move on to find the woman of his dreams who also had a similar vision as he did. The moral of my story: we go to the hairdresser's to cut off ends to enable more growth, and the same is applicable to relationships. Sure, this is maybe an example that will be better understood by women, but you get my point!

To know whether it is the right time to call things off, ask yourself the following: are you happy in your day-to-day life? Are you waking up, potentially next to this person, excited for the day to come? Have you been having great conversations lately, or has there been quite a bit of fighting? Do you still consider this person to be your best friend? When you think about the person you would like to spend the rest of your life with, so, when you think about future plans, marriage, kids, or even just going on a vacation, who is the person you picture yourself with?

I am guessing that by the time you are questioning your relationship, you must not be the happiest or must not be in the greatest place with your partner. So ask yourself this: what is the ratio of good times and bad times in your relationship? Do you still do exciting things together, or do you tend to mostly do the same routine? There is nothing wrong with routine, but ask yourself if your partner and/or you have the motivation to do something different together. For example, one of my best friends was dating someone for three years, and recently called it quits. When I asked her why, she told me that she was bored with the routine, and compared her relationship to her other friend's, explaining to me that they never do fun things together. For example, whereas her friend and their boyfriends would go out in the middle of the night and go for a Vespa tour, whenever she brought up the idea of doing some kind of date, her boyfriend would be too tired or simply uninterested. Therefore, if this is something you can relate to, maybe try to move things around and to bring back the spice by trying new things, but if you feel unmotivated or if your partner seems uninterested, it may be time to reconsider the relationship.

There are numerous other reasons as to why you could be considering calling off a relationship. However, do not let this discourage you. If one relationship does not work, it does not mean that you are doomed for life; you can find love elsewhere, as long as you put yourself out there and are open for other opportunities.

Breaking it off nicely

You may now wonder just how you can put an end to a relationship without hurting the other person too much. My tip on this is to be open, frank, and to get to the point. Do not lead the person on, once you have made the decision, bring it up in a nice way. If this person is someone you live with, keep in mind that you or they may need to move out. Also, think of the place you will call it off– in a restaurant on New Year's Eve is not the best time or place. Go for something that won't be a constant reminder of your breakup– you wouldn't like to have to think about your breakup for the next three New Year's Eves, would you? However, do not let it linger. Do it as soon as possible to spare some pain and anguish for the both of you. Of course, you do not *have* to give an explanation, but it may be best to give one to avoid late night, drunk calls from this woman trying to figure out why you dumped her. If she tries to contact you multiple times afterwards, try to cut out contact in a nice way by explaining that having space may be a good idea for both of you at first. All in all, I would suggest avoiding hurting her feelings as much as possible by being honest and showing that you care. If this is indeed someone that you still care about, maybe start it off by saying "I first want you to know that I deeply care about you", and maybe follow with something along the lines of "but this is not working, I am (insert unhappy/not ready to commit/not sure we are looking for the same thing, etc)".

Ultimately, the few things to keep in mind are as follows:

1. You will hurt the other person's feelings, no matter how hard you try not to.
2. Being honest is always better than making up a lie to spare the others' feelings.
3. Sooner is better.
4. Respect the other in terms of the time and place you choose to break things off.
5. You will find someone else! Don't stay in a bad relationship just because you are scared to be alone again.

I was dumped– how do I gain my confidence back?

This one is difficult. Dumping someone can really hurt, especially if you are breaking things off because you know it is for the best although you still love this person. But, being dumped, or broken up with, hurts even more, I think. So how can you keep the confidence you have built before, or rebuild it, once being dumped?

The first thing to mention is the following: being left by someone does not mean that there is something wrong with you. It means that the person did not want to have a relationship with you, which is different. We are all unique in our own ways, and there will always be someone that does not like you or a part of you, it's inevitable! So, this is something to keep in mind in any case. Additionally, I find that it is important to look at the relationship critically when getting over heartbreak. By this, I mean that you must stop only thinking about the positive, and that you must focus on the negative instead– I know, this is completely the opposite of everything I have told you so far, but hear me out. Instead of thinking of your nice dates and good times together, think of your disagreements, of the things that you disliked and of the reasons why your relationship ended up not working out.

You can work on acceptance later and on being friends with your ex one day (if this is something you wish), but first, concentrate on understanding why it didn't work out, and why you should be glad that it is over, and yes, this is difficult!

Moreover, allow yourself to mourn this relationship. Even if you were only dating this woman for two weeks, rejection hurts. Thus, allowing yourself to be sad about it coming to an end is perfectly normal and a very healthy thing to do. Cry it out, let out the emotions, and believe me, you will feel like a weight has been lifted off of your shoulders afterwards.

In order to rebuild your confidence, my tip is to put emphasis on those that love you and support you, therefore, spend time with loved ones and friends. Explain to them how you feel and make sure to let them know that you need more support than usual. If you prefer being alone, that's also completely understandable, but avoid isolating yourself for a long time. Seeing others and laughing is a cure for heartbreak. Similarly, if your goal is to build your confidence, use some of the tips I outlined earlier, but make sure to make your subconscious believe that you want to be confident. You can do this by dressing in a way that makes you feel your best and by concentrating on projects and routines that make you feel good. For example, if you love going to the gym because it makes you feel empowered afterwards, then do so and concentrate on bettering yourself. If seeking a revenge body is your motivation, then why not?

Things to keep in mind while going through a breakup is to let yourself feel, but not to let yourself fall down. By this, I mean be aware of the way you treat your mind and body. It's okay to go through a tub of ice cream once or twice at the beginning, but do not let it become a daily habit for months. Similarly, going out with friends is great, but do not let this turn into going out for drinks or using drugs in order to forget about the pain– this is a very slippery slope! You can find happiness again by finding healthy ways to cope, such as going boxing to get the anger out, or taking up a new hobby in order to get your mind off of things.

By using these tips, you should be able to slowly regain your confidence. In any case, the things to focus on are that you will not always feel this pain, that it is not you, who is the problem, but rather the relationship between you and your partner, that did not fit. Do not focus on the personal, but rather look for things to improve in the following relationships. Find something else to concentrate on, such as a new sport or a new hobby, rather than focusing on the reasons why this relationship failed and looking at it as if you were doomed forever. Finally, enjoy being single again once you have been able to move on slightly from this breakup, as it is something we do not learn to appreciate enough! I've already outlined to you why being single is great in the second chapter, so go check it out again if you are going through a breakup, or refer back to it if you are ever stuck facing one.

Over the course of this final chapter, we have taken the time to discuss breakups and failing relationships. Unfortunately, this is also an important part of dating as it is likely to happen, unless you are extremely lucky with love and are able to find your lifelong soulmate after a single date. Your confidence does not have to be broken even if you are facing a breakup, although rejection hurts anyone and makes one wonder *why* and *what it is about us that made it go wrong*. In any case, there are ways to rebuild it if it is hit hard. You will get through this, it's only another experience of life that we all go through, one way or another!

Conclusion

Over the course of our time together, we spent quite a bit of time looking into the different aspects that are involved in the art of dating. Who knew it was so complex? Indeed, finding the right woman to spend the rest of your life with is tricky– from building your confidence in order to approach women the right way, to understanding why it has become much more difficult to find love nowadays, to finding the right spot for the first date, and finally to figuring out how to break up with someone and how to get back up if we are the ones being broken up with, understanding dating and navigating through this process is complicated.

We began by taking a look at the history of dating, investigating why it has become so complex, and therefore having some insights as to what are the challenges we are facing today. Through this, I explained that commitment such as children and marriage are things the younger generations– yes Millennials, I'm looking at you!– seem to be avoiding or are reluctant to get into. I told you about online dating, the dark and complicated world that it is, however, this is something that you should be well-acquainted with by now!

Then, we looked at growing confidence and how important the latter is for a successful dating life. Being confident is one of the most desired traits by women when it comes to finding a partner; it is something very attractive. Additionally, your confidence is not limited to your love life, but to your work and social lives as well, and a greater confidence usually means a greater happiness in all spheres of life. Indeed, the more you love yourself, the higher your esteem, and the happier you can be.

Then, the third chapter was all about how your vibe attracts your tribe– the way you present yourself to others impacts how they see you in the end. Therefore, the happier you seem, the more confident and outgoing others see you, and the better are your chances of attracting someone that has similar qualities– the same *vibes*.

In the fourth chapter, we went down to business. We explored the places to find love, and where you have the most chances of finding someone you will really connect with based on your wishes and the other person's. Then, the fifth chapter took this a step further as we looked at approaching women; where to do so and when to avoid it. How to approach women in real life versus online, especially since these are completely different! On top of this, dating apps each differ and the demography you will deal with on the various platforms will require different types of messages and approaches.

Then, the sixth chapter focused on preparing you for the first date, or first few dates with the woman you have in mind. Finding a place that is in public to make sure she is comfortable, and making sure to keep the 'sex' topic for an appropriate time were two of the main points, so keep those in mind once you have successfully been able to make a connection with a woman– the next step is to ask her out, so refer back to this chapter!

And, finally, we went back down to Earth and spoke about an unfortunate reality: you may face heartbreak. It hurts and it sucks, if we are going to speak honestly! But there are ways to navigate through heartbreak, even if you were the one broken up with, to make sure that it does not completely break you and leave you back to where you started at the very beginning of this book. Thus, refer back to this chapter if you are unfortunately stuck in that situation… Hopefully, you will not need to!

Ultimately, my hope with this book was to help you better understand how women work, and how to date them successfully. Dating is complex, it requires work, but if it all works out in the end, then it is absolutely worth it. Thus, on this note, you are completely prepared for a successful dating life. You have all the information and tools necessary to go onto the dating scene and to find the right partner.

So what are you waiting for?